THE FABULOUS LOST & FOUND

AND THE LITTLE VIETNAMESE MOUSE

WRITTEN BY MARK PALLIS
ILLUSTRATED BY PETER BAYNTON

NEU WESTEND PRESS

For Jason - MP

For Hannah and Skye - PB

THE FABULOUS LOST & FOUND AND THE LITTLE VIETNAMESE MOUSE
Copyright text © 2020 Mark Pallis and Copyright images © 2020 Peter Baynton

All rights reserved. This book or any portion thereof may not be reproduced or used in any manner whatsoever without the express written permission of the publisher except for the use of brief excerpts in a review.

First Printing, 2020
ISBN: 978-1-913595-20-3
NeuWestendPress.com

THE FABULOUS LOST & FOUND

AND THE LITTLE VIETNAMESE MOUSE

WRITTEN BY MARK PALLIS
ILLUSTRATED BY PETER BAYNTON

NEU WESTEND
— PRESS —

In the middle of the big city is a tiny yellow building. If anyone loses anything, this is where it ends up.

It is called the Lost and Found.

Mr and Mrs Frog keep everything safe, hoping that someday every lost watch and bag and phone and toy and shoe and cheesegrater will find its owner again.

But the shop is very small. And there are so many lost things. It is all quite a squeeze, but still, it's fabulous.

One sunny day, a little mouse walked in.

"Welcome," said Mrs Frog. "What have you lost?"

"Tôi bị mất mũ," said the mouse.

Mr and Mrs Frog could not speak Vietnamese. They had no idea what the little mouse was saying.

What shall we do? they wondered.

Maybe she's lost an umbrella. Everyone loses an umbrella at least twice, thought Mr Frog.

"Have you lost this?" asked Mr Frog.

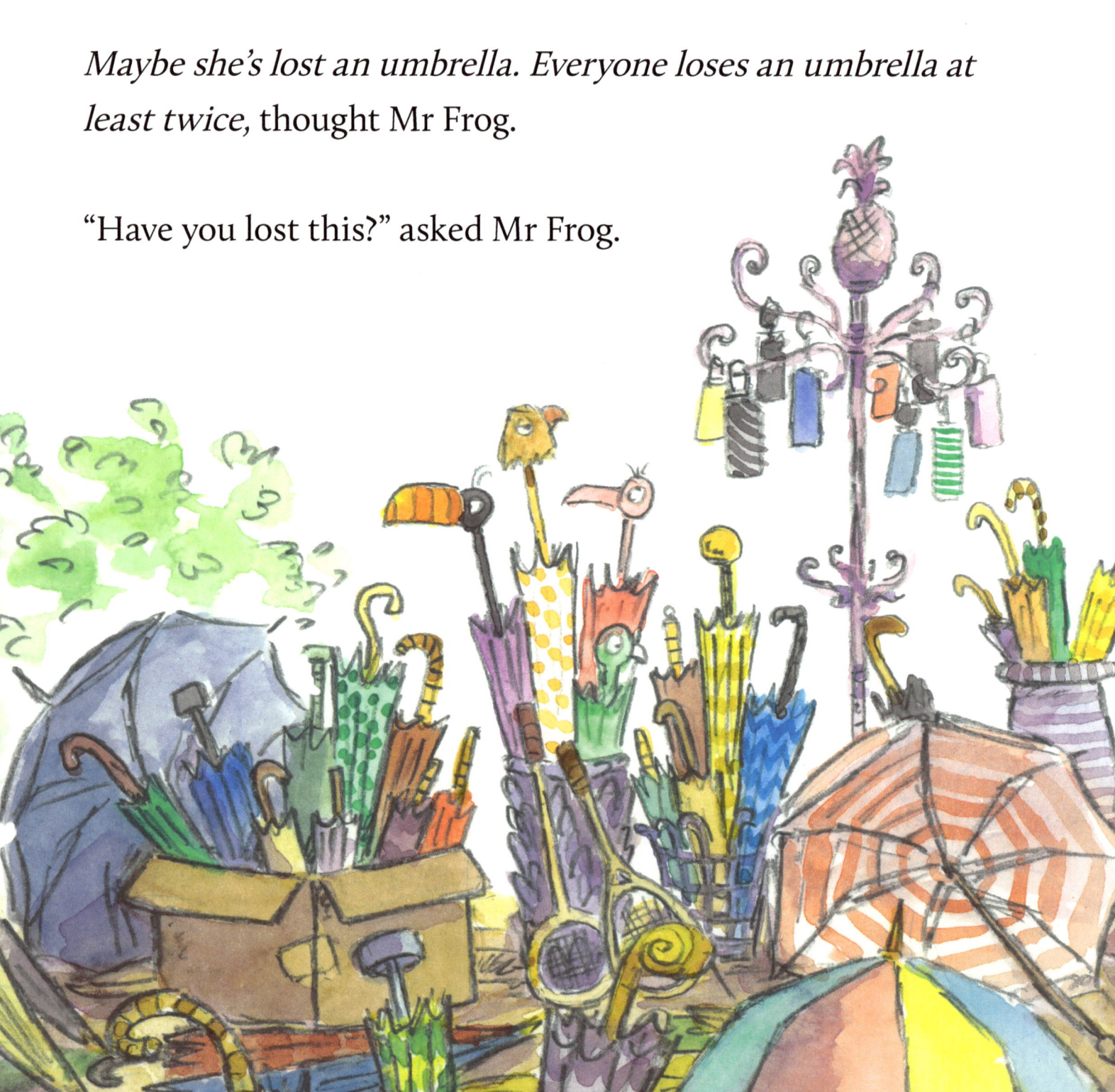

"Cái dù? Không," replied the mouse.

Then Mrs Frog remembered something that had been handed in a few months ago…

"Is this yours?" Mrs Frog asked, holding up a chunk of cheese.

"Phô mai? Không. Nó bốc mùi!" said the mouse.

"Time to put that cheese in the bin dear," said Mr Frog.

"Maybe the word 'mũ' means coat," said Mr Frog.

"Now where did I put that nice yellow one?"

"Got it!" said Mr Frog.

"Một chiếc áo choàng? Không.

Tôi bị mất mũ," said the mouse.

She was starting to feel a bit frustrated.

"We need to keep trying," said Mrs Frog.

Không phải là khăn quàng.

Không phải là quần dài.

Không phải là áo len.

Không phải là kính râm.

Không phải là đôi giày.

"Tôi bị mất mũ," said the mouse.

Không phải hai chiếc xe đạp.

Không phải cái máy tính.

Không phải ba cuốn sách.

Không phải bốn quả chuối.

Không phải năm chìa khóa.

It was no good. A fat wet tear rolled down the mouse's cheek.

"How about a nice cup of tea?" asked Mrs Frog kindly.

"Tôi thích uống trà. Cảm ơn," replied the mouse.
They sat together, sipping their tea and all feeling a bit sad.

Suddenly, the mouse realised she could try pointing.

She pointed at her head.
"Mũ!" she said.

"I've got it!" exclaimed Mrs Frog, leaping up.

"A wig of course!" said Mrs Frog.

"Không phải tóc giả," said the mouse.

Không phải tóc đỏ.

Không phải tóc vàng hoe.

Không màu nâu.

Không nhiều màu.

Không phải mầu xanh lá cây.

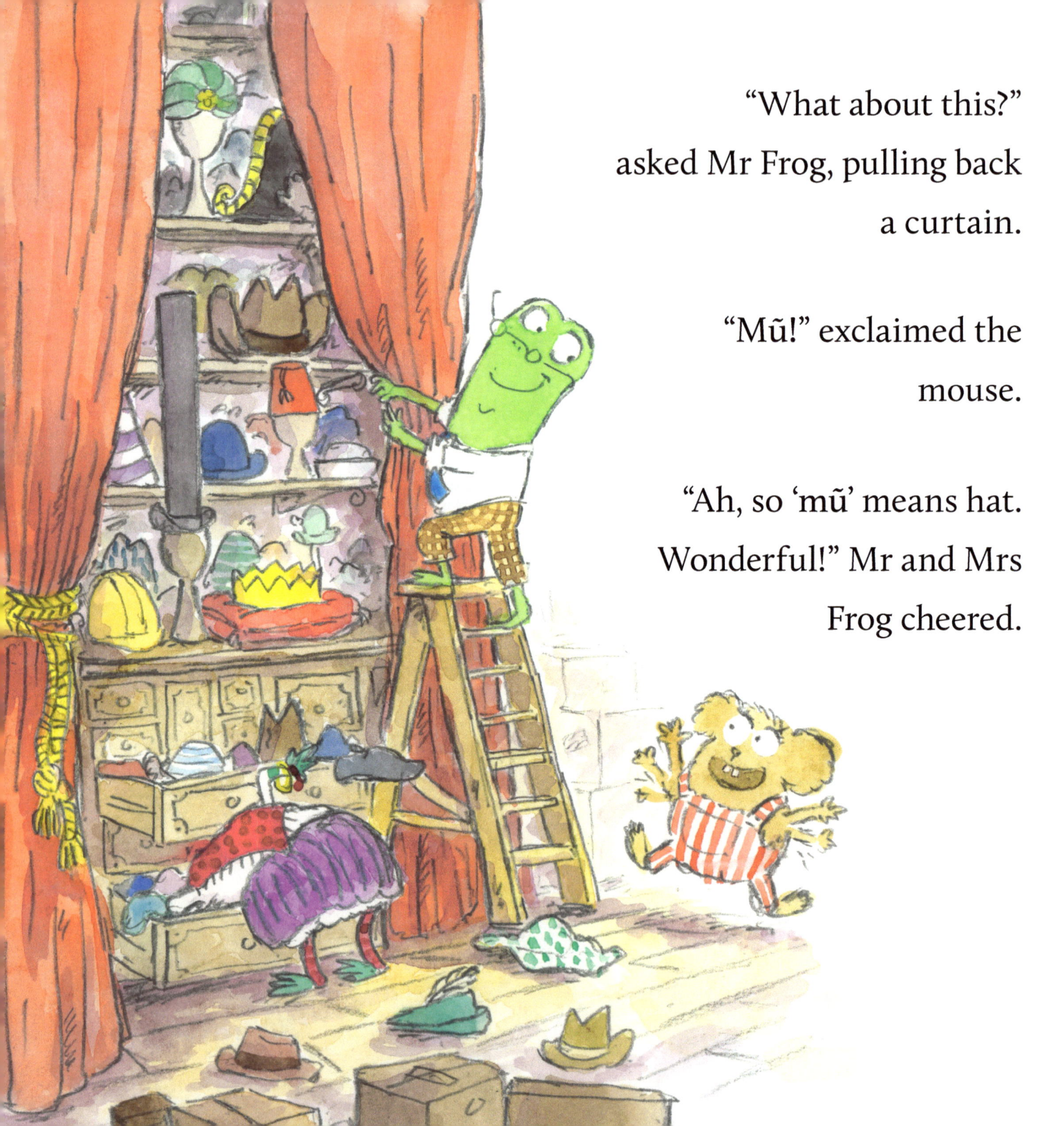

"What about this?" asked Mr Frog, pulling back a curtain.

"Mũ!" exclaimed the mouse.

"Ah, so 'mũ' means hat. Wonderful!" Mr and Mrs Frog cheered.

Quá cao.

Quá nhỏ.

Quá to.

Quá chật.

"One hat left," said Mrs Frog, reaching all the way to the back of the cupboard.

"It couldn't be this old thing, could it?"

"Mũ của tôi.

Tôi đã tìm thấy cái mũ của tôi!

Cảm ơn rất nhiều," said the mouse.

And just like that, the mouse found her hat.

"Tạm biệt," she said, as she skipped away.
"Tạm biệt," replied Mr and Mrs Frog.

"I wonder who will come tomorrow?" said Mr Frog. Mrs Frog put her arm around him. "I don't know," she replied, giving him a squeeze, "but whoever it is, we'll do our best to help."

LEARNING TO LOVE LANGUAGES

An additional language opens a child's mind, broadens their horizons and enriches their emotional life. Research has shown that the time between a child's birth and their sixth or seventh birthday is a "golden period" when they are most receptive to new languages. This is because they have an in-built ability to distinguish the sounds they hear and make sense of them. The Story-powered Language Learning Method taps into these natural abilities.

HOW THE STORY-POWERED LANGUAGE LEARNING METHOD WORKS

We create an emotionally engaging and funny story for children and adults to enjoy together, just like any other picture book. Studies show that social interaction, like enjoying a book together, is critical in language learning.

Through the story, we introduce a relatable character who speaks only in the new language. This helps build empathy and a positive attitude towards people who speak different languages. These are both important aspects in laying the foundations for lasting language acquisition in a child's life.

As the story progresses, the child naturally works with the characters to discover the meanings of a wide range of fun new words. Strategic use of humour ensures that this subconscious learning is rewarded with laughter; the child feels good and the first seeds of a lifelong love of languages are sown.

For more information and free downloads visit www.neuwestendpress.com

ALL THE BEAUTIFUL VIETNAMESE WORDS AND PHRASES FROM OUR STORY

tôi bị mất mũ	I've lost my hat
cái dù	umbrella
phô mai	cheese
nó bốc mùi	it stinks
áo choàng	coat
khăn quàng	scarf
quần	trousers
kính râm	sunglasses
áo len	sweater
giày	shoe
một	one
hai	two
ba	three
bốn	four
năm	five
máy tính	computer
sách	book
chìa khóa	key
chuối	banana
xe đạp	bicycle
tôi thích trà	I love tea
cảm ơn	thank you
tóc giả	wig
đỏ	red
tóc vàng hoe	blond
màu nâu	brown
xanh lá cây	green
nhiều màu	multicoloured
mũ	hat
quá cao	too tall
quá to	too big
quá nhỏ	too small
quá chật	too tight
tôi đã tìm thấy cái mũ của tôi	I've found my hat
cảm ơn rất nhiều	thank you very much
tạm biệt	goodbye